POO DOWN UNDER

by
John Wood

Minneapolis, Minnesota

Credits:
All images are courtesy of Shutterstock.com, unless otherwise specified. With thanks to Getty Images, Thinkstock Photo, and iStockphoto.

Front Cover – johavel, shaineast. Title typeface used throughout – PremiumVector. Vector flies – Top Vector Studio. 2 – ooodles. 4–5 – Daria Nipot, Travelling.About, nataliia pshenychna. 6–7 – Eric Isselee, ChameleonsEye, S_Images.com, Phassa K, Gurza. 8–9 – Farjana.rahman, Spill Photography, Usagi-P, baldezh, iuliia_n. 10–11 – dwi putra stock, dwi putra stock, dwi putra stock, Henk Vrieselaar. 12–13 – Benny Marty, Geoff Shaw, CC BY-SA 3.0 <http://creativecommons.org/licenses/by-sa/3.0/>, via Wikimedia Commons, Evgeniia Mokeeva, nataliia pshenychna, Colorfuel Studio. 14–15 – Daria Nipot, Travelling.About. 16–17 – james_stone76, Miela197, Maquiladora, VectorShow. 18–19 – Eric Isselee, GoodFocused, charnsitr. 20–21 – Martin Pelanek, Susan Flashman, Sko Helen, Amanita Silvicora. 22–23 – Susan Flashman, Mandy Creighton, StockSmartStart.

Bearport Publishing Company Product Development Team
Publisher: Jen Jenson; Director of Product Development: Spencer Brinker; Managing Editor: Allison Juda; Editor: Cole Nelson; Associate Editor: Naomi Reich; Associate Editor: Tiana Tran; Art Director: Colin O'Dea; Designer: Kim Jones; Designer: Kayla Eggert; Product Development Specialist: Owen Hamlin

Library of Congress Cataloging-in-Publication Data is available at www.loc.gov or upon request from the publisher.

ISBN: 979-8-89232-751-0 (hardcover)
ISBN: 979-8-89232-801-2 (paperback)
ISBN: 979-8-89232-838-8 (ebook)

© 2025 BookLife Publishing
This edition is published by arrangement with BookLife Publishing.

North American adaptations © 2025 Bearport Publishing Company. All rights reserved. No part of this publication may be reproduced in whole or in part, stored in any retrieval system, or transmitted in any form or by any means, electronic, mechanical, photocopying, recording, or otherwise, without written permission from the publisher.

For more information, write to Bearport Publishing, 5357 Penn Avenue South, Minneapolis, MN 55419.

CONTENTS

All About Poo 4
Don't Eat These Greens 6
Dark Droppings 10
White Poo 14
Grassy and in Groups 18
Bonus Poo! 22
Glossary 24
Index 24

ALL ABOUT POO

Many **unique** animals live in Australia. And their poo is just as special. Let's take a look at who poos Down Under!

An animal's poo tells you a lot about it.

Don't touch any poo you find Down Under. Poo has lots of nasty things in it!

On the next pages, you will see poo found in Australia. Learn all about that poo, and choose which animal you think made it. Then, turn the page to see if you were right!

DON'T EAT THESE GREENS

This poo looks and smells interesting. Whose is it?

This poo is small. The **pellets** are about the size of a grape.

The poo is dark green. This animal must eat a lot of green plants.

WHOSE POO WAS IT?

I eat a lot, so I poo a lot. It's not my fault!

It was the koala's POO!

Koalas eat the leaves of **eucalyptus** (*yoo*-kuh-LIP-tuhs) trees. This is what makes their poo green. The leafy food also gives the poo its smell.

Baby koalas are called joeys. Instead of eating leaves, young joeys eat their mothers' poo! This special poo is known as pap.

Koalas poo up to 360 pellets a day. They even poo while sleeping!

Eating pap helps a joey's body get used to eucalyptus leaves. This allows the joey to eat the leaves once they are older.

DARK DROPPINGS

Look at this pile of poo. Whose poo is it?

There are many of these little poos in a line.

These pellets are shaped like uneven balls.

WHOSE POO WAS IT?

It was the **kangaroo's POO!**

It was me. I did the poo.

Mom, that stinks!

Kangaroos are **herbivores**. They eat only plants, such as grass, moss, and flowers. Often, the grass that they eat can be seen inside their poo.

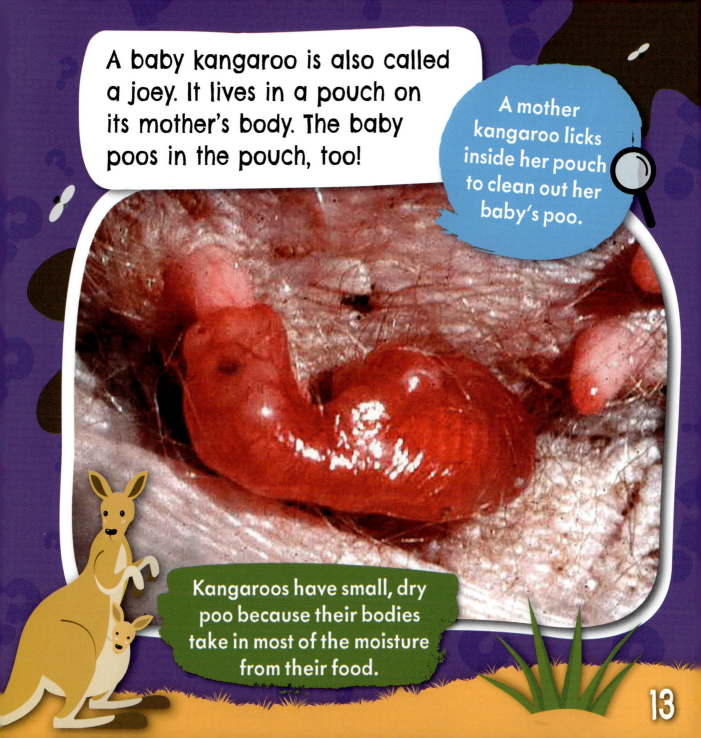

WHITE POO

Get a load of this poo! Who left it behind?

How unusual! This poo is white. That means there is a lot of **calcium** in the poo.

There are lots of these poos in one place. This is probably a shared toilet.

14

WHOSE POO WAS IT?

It was the Tasmanian devil's POO!

It's not all from me. That's a shared toilet!

Tasmanian devils eat other animals. Their powerful jaws let them crunch through animal bones. Calcium from the bones is what makes their poo white.

Groups of Tasmanian devils poo in special areas called **latrines**. They use latrines as a way to **communicate**. They smell the different poos to learn about who is nearby.

Bones and fur are hard to **digest**. So, they come out in the Tasmanian devil's poo.

GRASSY AND IN GROUPS

There are pellets everywhere. Who pooed and ran?

This poo looks a bit like a kangaroo's, but it is smaller.

There are bits of grass inside the poo.

The black pellets are in little piles.

WHOSE POO WAS IT?

It was the wallaby's POO!

I did it. But I didn't run away. I hopped!

Wallabies are a lot like kangaroos but smaller. They eat mostly grasses, leafy plants, and roots. Wallabies have large, flat teeth that help them chew their food.

Like baby kangaroos, wallaby babies live and poo in their mothers' pouches.

Wallabies use their noses to sniff out food they can't see. Then, they quickly hop toward their next snack.

Wallabies chew their food twice! They start by eating some food. Then, they throw up that food into their mouths and chew it again. This helps them get all the **nutrients**.

BONUS POO!

IT'S GOT TO BE CUBE

Wombats are probably best known for a strange fact about their poo. They are the only animals in the world that have cube-shaped poo!

My poos may be strange, but they are useful, too!

Wombats can drop up to 100 poo cubes a day. They use the cubes to mark their territory and communicate with other wombats. The flat sides keep the poos in place.

Wombats spend most of their time eating grass, moss, and other plants.

It can take up to 18 days for wombats to digest food. This is why their poo is very dry and hard.

GLOSSARY

calcium something in teeth, bones, and shells that makes these things hard and strong

communicate to pass information between two or more things

digest to break down food into things that can be used by the body

eucalyptus a type of tree in Australia

herbivores animals that eat only plants

latrines shared toilets

nutrients natural substances that plants and animals need to grow and stay healthy

pellets small, hard balls of poop or undigested food

unique special and unlike anything else

INDEX

babies 9, 13, 21
bones 15–17
fur 15, 17
groups 17–18
latrines 17
leaves 8–9, 20
nutrients 21
pap 9
pellets 6, 9–11, 18
plants 6, 12, 20, 23
pouches 13, 21